A Christmas Story of Light

For our favorite loves!

For Harvey, Charles, Pepper, and those grandchildren yet to come.
My deep gratitude to my sister, Christi Hydrick, for her never-ending support.

the Light(s) of our lives!

Published by Lighten Press

A Christmas Story of Light/ Ora Smith
ISBN : 978-0-9980410-1-8
Library of Congress Control Number: 2018913529
Art Consultant: Sarah Clemens
Photographer of Art: Emily Kellett of ENK'D
Editor: Lori Freeland
Layout and Design Adrienne Quintana of Pink Umbrella Books

♡ Love you Forever,
♡ Nana + Poppop
♡ 12/'22

written and illustrated by
Ora Smith

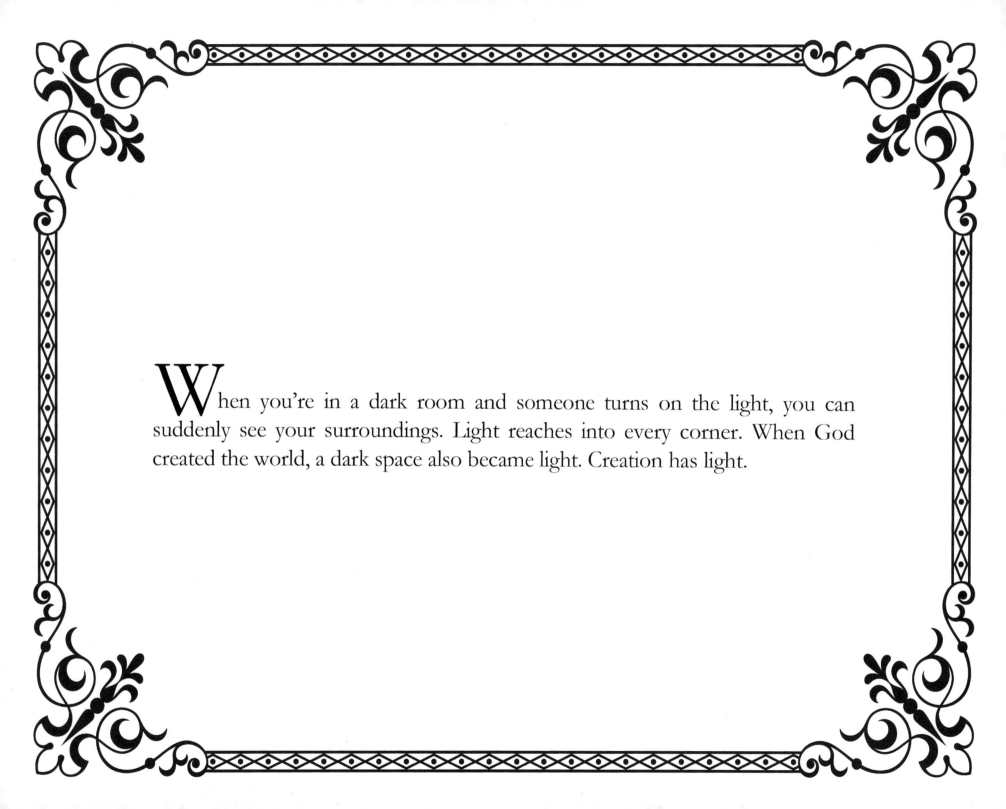

When you're in a dark room and someone turns on the light, you can suddenly see your surroundings. Light reaches into every corner. When God created the world, a dark space also became light. Creation has light.

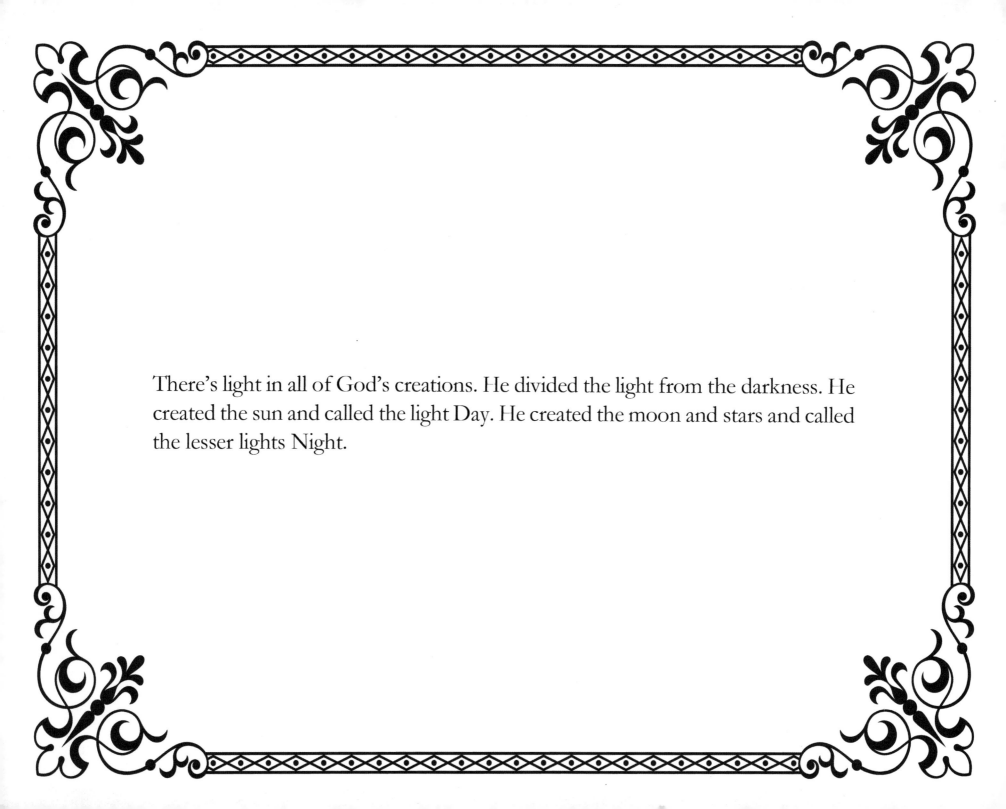

There's light in all of God's creations. He divided the light from the darkness. He created the sun and called the light Day. He created the moon and stars and called the lesser lights Night.

God created our beautiful planet as a gift, a place where we can grow, learn, love, and help others grow, learn, and love. Someday, God wants us to live with Him where His home is filled with more light than we have on earth.

Because God wants to bring us to His glorious home, He sent His son to lead the way. Jesus came to earth as a baby. He is the son of God and a woman named Mary, who lived more than two thousand years ago. She was engaged to a man named Joseph. One day, an angel named Gabriel came to Mary and told her she was special to God and would be the mother of Jesus.

Just before Jesus was born, Mary traveled to Bethlehem with her husband, Joseph, to pay taxes. The city was crowded. The inn where people stayed was full. When it was time for Jesus to be born, Mary gave birth in a stable where animals live.

Close to Bethlehem, shepherds watched over their lambs. An angel appeared to them in a light so bright it shone into the countryside. This was God's light, a heavenly light that displayed His glory. God's light can be hard for our eyes to behold.

The angel had an important message for the shepherds. He told them, "For unto you is born this day in the city of David a Savior, which is Christ the Lord. And this shall be a sign unto you: Ye shall find the babe wrapped in swaddling clothes, lying in a manger." Suddenly, many more angels joined him, praising God and saying, "Glory to God in the highest, and on earth peace, good will toward men."

The night Jesus was born, a new star shone brighter than any other. It was so bright, everyone in the whole world could see it. God sent it as a sign to represent the new light that had come into the world. Jesus is known as the Light of the World. This means when truth is presented, the Light of Christ will help you know it is right. The Light of Christ can also help you understand what is bad and what is good.

Three wise men from the East followed the star to where Jesus lived. When they found Him, they knelt and worshipped Jesus, then gave Him their treasures of gold, frankincense, and myrrh.

As a baby, Jesus's parents took him to the temple. A good man named Simeon blessed Jesus and said He would be "a light to lighten" the people. Simeon was right. When Jesus grew up, He taught peace and goodwill. If you learn and accept what He taught, you will find joy.

They didn't have cameras when Jesus lived. Instead, artists painted pictures of people. The oldest paintings of Jesus show rays of light around him. Light shining from someone is sometimes called a halo. It represents holiness, divine importance, power, or majesty.

There will always be light. Light can grow brighter and brighter and make darkness vanish. If you are having problems or if someone is hurting your feelings, you can call on God to assist you in being strong. He can give you the light of peace.

God sent Jesus to guide us. He wants you to show His light by being kind and helping others. Then you'll have your own light.

Don't hide your light. Let everyone see it. They see your light when you make them feel better if they are hurt, or when you help them do something they can't do by themselves. If you let your belief of Jesus burn brightly, you can make the world better with your light. Jesus said, "I am the light of the world: he that follows me shall not walk in darkness, but shall have the light of life."

There's a story in the Bible about ten young women who had never been married. These women were invited to a wedding feast. In those days they didn't have electricity like we do. They used fire for light. The feast was to take place at night, so they needed to have enough oil in their lamps to keep a flame burning to find their way in the dark. Five of the young women did not prepare ahead and didn't have enough oil, which made them late to the feast. The five who had enough oil lit their way to the bridegroom and made it to the feast before the doors were closed behind them. Once the doors were closed, no one else could come in, including the five women who had no light and were late.

The story is called a parable. That means it's a story that teaches us something. The bridegroom is really Jesus, and the unmarried women are His followers. By having our own light, we will be Jesus's followers also. The parable is a warning that we need to be ready with our light of goodness for when Christ comes to earth again.

We can't see very well in the dark. Without light, we might not see dangers in our path. God's light allows us to see things clearly. This same light gives us a brightness of hope so we can believe all will work out for the best. Right now, you may only "feel" Jesus's light. But God promised Jesus would return to earth. Like a match struck in darkness, when Jesus's light shines again, all people will see it.

Because everything God creates has light, you have light too. God created your spirit. You are His child. All people were created by God before they were born on earth. That's why we call Him our Heavenly Father. Before you came to earth into a body, you lived in His home of light.

Your physical body is made up of atoms. As long as you are alive, your atoms emit light. There are seven billion billion billion of them lighting up your body. If you looked through a special microscope, you could see the flashes of light happening in your atoms. You are a physical being of light.

At Christmastime there are many stories and decorations to remind you of Jesus Christ, the Light of the World. Think of Him when you see lights sparkling on a house, or wrapped around your Christmas tree, or brightening the nativity scene with baby Jesus in a manger.

The most important thing to remember is that God sent Jesus Christ to earth to redeem us. That means through His atonement you can live with God forever in His light, where you will be happier than you've ever been.

This book was inspired by my desire to teach my grandchildren what I hold most precious in my heart—my testimony of God and His son, Jesus Christ.

Grandkids are "bright lights" in my life.

CPSIA information can be obtained at www.ICGtesting.com
Printed in the USA
LVIW010249041120
670656LV00013B/122